CONTENTS

MEET MERLE

Merle is our family's youngest member. He was adopted from the Ingham County Animal Control Shelter in Mason, Michigan, surrendered there because the owner had too many dogs. His history was unknown when we adopted him, but we have learned that he is a mix of Boston terrier, cocker spaniel, Pekingese, and Australian shepherd. It's true—his ears are really, really big! He has been my quilting companion throughout this project. He will be your companion, too, as you "paw" through the pages of this book.

Located...
Society...
ments...
events, AQS strives to honor today's quiltmakers and their work and to inspire future creativity and innovation in quiltmaking.

EXECUTIVE EDITOR: ELAINE H. BRELSFORD
BOOK EDITOR: LINDA BAXTER LASCO
COPY EDITOR: CHRYSTAL ABHALTER
GRAPHIC DESIGN: JEFFREY BECK
QUILT PHOTOGRAPHY: CHARLES R. LYNCH
ADDITIONAL PHOTOGRAPHY: KAREN DULING

Library of Congress Cataloging-in-Publication Data

Duling, Karen.
   Quilting for the paws / by Karen Duling.
      pages cm
   ISBN 978-1-60460-148-0
   1. Patchwork--Patterns. 2. Quilting--Patterns. 3. Decoration and ornament--Animal forms. I. Title.
   TT835.D87 2014
   746.46'041--dc23

                          2013036117

Additional copies of this book may be ordered from the American Quilter's Society, PO Box 3290, Paducah, KY 42002-3290, or online at www.AmericanQuilter.com.

Attention Photocopying Service: Please note the following — Publisher and author give permission to print pages 10, 11, 29, and 30 for personal use only.

Dedication & Acknowledgments

This book is dedicated to animal shelter staff and volunteers. The county shelter in my area, serving the medium-sized community of Lansing, Michigan, cares for approximately 5,700 animals each year, providing needed medical treatment, food, and shelter as it seeks to place them in suitable homes. May good things come to animal shelters, pets, and pet owners as a result of quilts made from this book.

A big "Thank You!" goes out to my sister, Cindy Bowker, for introducing me to the wonderful world of fabric and sewing. Cindy and I have been fortunate to share time with Gwen Marston at her Beaver Island Quilt Retreats. Gwen's advocacy has been the key to the success of this project. She has been with me throughout, providing advice and encouragement. Paula Clegg of St. James City, Florida, has been my "agent," inspiring me through her love for dogs and spreading the word about my work. My husband, Linn, has made this project easier by cheerfully tolerating my days in the quilt room and helping with equipment issues. Thank you for your love and support, Linn!

LUCKY DOG, 47" x 47", Karen Duling and Cindy Bowker. Machine quilting by Wendy Paskus, East Lansing, Michigan. Donated to the Ingham County Animal Shelter, Mason, Michigan.

Introduction to Paw & Tail Quilts

I love making quilts about dogs and cats. I started making them as fund-raising items for my community animal shelter. After a bit, I learned that these quilts also make thoughtful gifts for those who are grieving from the loss of a pet. I have given them as baby gifts, made them to warm the bed of a child, and I have made them simply to celebrate the joy of having a dog or cat. I hope this book will inspire you to make these quilts, too.

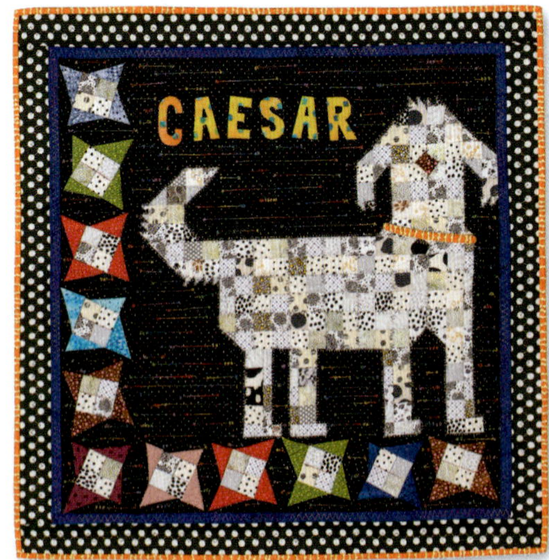

CAESAR, 2011, 28" x 28"
Made for our wonderful English setter.

FABRICS

Since I started making paw and tail quilts, my quilting and fabric collecting have become more focused and more fun. It's like being on a treasure hunt, searching quilt shops for that special pet-themed fabric to add to my collection. Many times, these fabrics serve as a creative launch for my next quilt design (FIG. 1).

Paw-print and pet-themed fabrics add whimsy to the quilt projects. Paw prints are the animal lover's version of polka dots! You may be surprised how easy it is to find these at your local quilt shop. Finding them in the color that coordinates with other fabrics can be a bit more challenging. If you are unsuccessful finding them locally, try these online sources. Enter "paw print" or "dog bone" or another such phrase in the search box. Items in their fabric inventory will be displayed for your shopping pleasure.

www.creativequiltkits.com
www.equilter.com
www.fatquartershop.com
www.hawthornethreads.com
www.quilthome.com
www.spoonflower.com—A huge selection of fabric designs that can be custom ordered to print on Kona® cotton or a variety of other fabrics.

Quality 100 percent cotton quilting fabrics will make your sewing experience more pleasurable and add to the lasting value of your project.

Each year, a few designers will release a collection of coordinating pet-themed fabrics, simplifying the fabric selection process. The most important concept when selecting fabric for these projects is to choose a range of colors that includes light, dark, and medium values.

I enjoy combining fabrics from many collections with fabrics from my stash to add that little bit of the unexpected in each quilt. For me, playing with the fabrics and the colors is the most fun of all the quiltmaking steps.

FIG. 1. My paw-print fabric stash.

SUPPLIES

You need basic quilting supplies to make the quilts in this book: rotary cutter; self-healing cutting mat; clear plastic quilting ruler; iron and ironing surface; fine straight pins; sewing machine and appropriately sized sharp machine needles for the thread being used; sewing thread; scissors for paper and fabric; seam ripper and fabric marking pencil. Spray starch is helpful to stabilize fabric before applying fusible web.

If accurate ¼" seams have been a problem area for you, a sewing machine foot with a ¼" seam guide may be helpful.

BASICS

This book focuses on quilt patterns, project-specific instructions, advice, and resources. General quiltmaking instructions can be found on the AQS website at www.americanquilter.com; enter "quiltmaking essentials" in the search box.

Quilt sizes in the project instructions are pieced quilt top dimensions before quilting. Patterns assume 40" usable width of fabric. Strips are cut across the width of fabric from selvage to selvage.

Machine Appliqué

Appliqué pieces in the projects are made using paper-backed fusible web—a thin adhesive sheet that joins two layers of fabric when heated with your iron. Choose a lightweight paper-backed fusible web such as Lite Steam-A-Seam 2. Follow manufacturer's directions for iron settings and length of time for fusing.

After fusing, use the stitch of your choice to sew around the shapes, always stitching on the top fabric to provide a nice finished edge. Options include the blanket, zigzag, and straight stitch. If preferred, this step can be done after all the quilt layers are assembled and used as part of the quilting design.

MERLE'S TIPS!

I like to use a zigzag stitch with MonoPoly™ from Superior Threads for the top thread, a size 70 topstitch needle, my regular sewing thread in the bobbin, and a stitch length and width of 1.8 mm.

If you choose to use a different appliqué method, note that seam allowances are not included on appliqué template patterns.

Half-Square Triangle Units (HSTs)

Select two fabric squares ⅞" larger than your desired FINISHED size. Place right sides together with the edges matching. Using a fabric marking pencil, draw a diagonal line from one corner to the opposite corner on the wrong side of the lighter fabric.

Sew two seams, each ¼" from the diagonal line. Use your rotary cutter or scissors to cut through both layers of fabric on the drawn line.

Press open, pressing the seam toward the darker fabric. You'll have two HSTs! Trim the points so that you have squares of the desired size.

When starting out, check your finished HSTs to see that they do indeed finish at the desired size. If they do not, try starching the fabric before cutting and sewing. It helps to stabilize the threads and minimize distortion. I like using Mary Ellen's Best Press™ Spray Starch (maryellenproducts.com). Double-check your seam allowance to make sure it is ¼". Take care when pressing that you are not pulling the fabric and distorting the square.

If you are still having trouble creating an accurately sized HST, consider cutting the originating fabric squares a bit larger, and then trimming the HSTs to the exact size required. An acrylic ruler tool from Bloc Loc is wonderful for cutting down HSTs to the desired size (www.blocloc.com). Using a rotating cutting mat with the Bloc Loc ruler is the cherry on top!

Borders

Sew long border strips together from end to end and press the seams open. Lay the strip over the center of the quilt from top to bottom. Cut two pieces to this exact length for the side borders.

If your pattern calls for cornerstones, lay the remaining strip over the center of the quilt from side to side. Cut two pieces to that size. Add the cornerstones to each end for the top and bottom borders. Press toward the border strip.

If there are no cornerstones, add the side borders before measuring and cutting the top and bottom borders.

Add the side borders first, then the top and bottom borders, pinning to evenly ease any fullness.

It's time to make the projects!

Black Cats and Black Dogs: Wallhanging Projects

BLACK CATS, 24" x 45", made by the author

BLACK DOGS, 24" x 45", made by the author. Machine quilting by Wendy Paskus, East Lansing, Michigan.

Pattern Inspiration

This quilt pattern celebrates black cats and black dogs—often the last ones to be adopted at the animal shelter. Black cat, Fritz and Black Lab, Biaka, inspired the design. Fritz had been abandoned in a brown paper bag on a city bus before being rescued.

BLACK CATS, 24" x 45", by Jessica Ratliff, DeWitt, Michigan

O IS FOR OTIS, 24" x 45", by Cindy Bowker, Bozeman, Montana

This pattern works with a variety of fabrics. Jessica Ratliff used black cats with gray and yellow prints. She also added embellishments to make collars and eyes.

Cindy Bowker chose a colorway that goes nicely with her dog, Otis. She shows that the dogs don't even need to be facing the same direction.

Cindy Bowker's dog, Otis.

Karen Duling

YARDAGE REQUIREMENTS
for Finished Size 24" x 45"

Color values should range from light to dark. I like to use hand-dyed fabrics because of the intensity of the colors. In the sample, approximately ⅓ of the squares are black and ⅓ are light/neutral in color. Read the cutting instructions before purchasing fabric.

Assorted scraps for half-square triangle units (HSTs)	You need 153 squares at least 2⅞" x 2⅞".
Black fabric for the animals	½ yard
Background rectangle for the animals	6 assorted fat eighths* (approximately 11" x 18")
Top border strip	⅛ yard
Bottom border strip	⅛ yard
Binding	⅜ yard
Batting	32" x 53"
Backing	1½ yards
Paper-backed fusible web	1½ yards**

*After cutting background rectangles from fat eighths, use the remaining fabric to add to the assortment of fabrics for the half-square triangles.

** It is best to use yardage rather than sheets for this project as some of the animal shapes are larger than the precut sheets.

CUTTING AND TEMPLATE INSTRUCTIONS
for Dog or Cat

Enlarge or reduce the animal template by the percentages shown.

Exact cut sizes for the squares to make HSTs are given in the chart. An easier option is to cut all 153 squares 2⅞" x 2⅞". Assemble the HSTs (page 4), then trim the appropriate number of units down to the unfinished sizes shown in the chart. This assures greater accuracy in the sizes of the HSTs, although it does use just a bit more fabric. The up side is that all pieces fit very nicely together when the HSTs are precisely the sizes shown, and it allows you to play with the placement of the HSTs before committing them to a certain location.

	Animal 1	Animal 2	Animal 3	Animal 4	Animal 5	Animal 6
Animal template	60%	80%	100%	120%	133%	150%
Background rectangles	4¼" x 14"	6" x 13"	6½" x 13½"	8⅝" x 15⅞"	9¼" x 17"	9⅞" x 16½"
HST units needed	26 – 2⅛" x 2⅛"	32 – 2¼" x 2¼"	28 – 2⅜" x 2⅜"	25 – 2½" x 2½"	20 – 2⅝" x 2⅝"	22 – 2¾" x 2¾"
Unfinished HSTs: size	1¾"	1⅞"	2"	2⅛"	2¼"	2⅜"

Top border 1¾" x 21½" **Bottom border** 2⅜" x 20¼"
Two of the largest and two of the smallest HSTs are sewn to the border strips for cornerstones.

SEWING INSTRUCTIONS

Read through all instructions before cutting. They are the same whether you choose the cat or dog shape. Pick your favorite and start creating!

STEP 1: Enlarge or reduce animal shapes to the sizes shown on the cutting instructions chart to make six animal pattern pieces. The finished animals will be mirror images of the pattern pieces.

STEP 2: Trace each animal pattern onto the paper side of the fusible web. Cut approximately ⅜" OUTSIDE of the drawn line. Then cut roughly ¼" INSIDE the traced line. It is okay to cut right through the traced line to get to the inside of the animal pattern for cutting. The purpose of cutting away the fusible web on the inside is to finish with a quilt block that is as soft and flexible as possible.

STEP 3: Place the fusible animal shapes onto the back of your black fabric paper-side up, taking care not to distort the animal shape. Following manufacturer's directions, fuse in place (**FIG. 2**).

STEP 4: Cut out on the traced line (**FIG. 3A**).

Remove the paper backing. With animals now facing to the right, visually center each animal on the right side of the appropriate background rectangle (**FIG. 3B**). Fuse in place. Machine appliqué to provide a nice finished edge (page 4).

STEP 5: Assemble and sew HSTs in the quantity shown for each size (page 7).

STEP 6: Lay out the HSTs according to the placement illustration on page 9. Sew HSTs together in rows for each Unit A and Unit C. Press in the directions shown. Then sew rows together to complete an A and C unit for each animal. Sew A and C units to the appropriate animal background rectangle (Unit B).

STEP 7: Sew completed A, B, and C unit strips to one another.

STEP 8: Add the top and bottom borders. Use two HSTs as cornerstones on each border piece. Position the

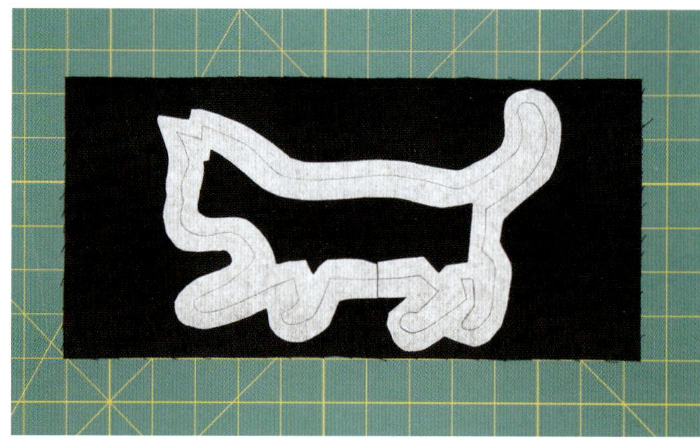

FIG. 2. The traced and trimmed shape fused to the wrong side of the animal fabric.

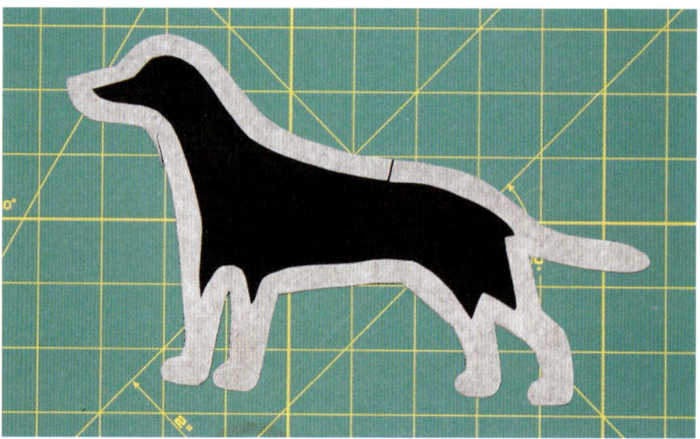

FIG. 3A. The cut out animal shape

FIG. 3B. The finished rectangle

cornerstone HSTs so that the darker triangle frames each corner of the quilt.

STEP 9: Assemble quilt layers and quilt as desired.

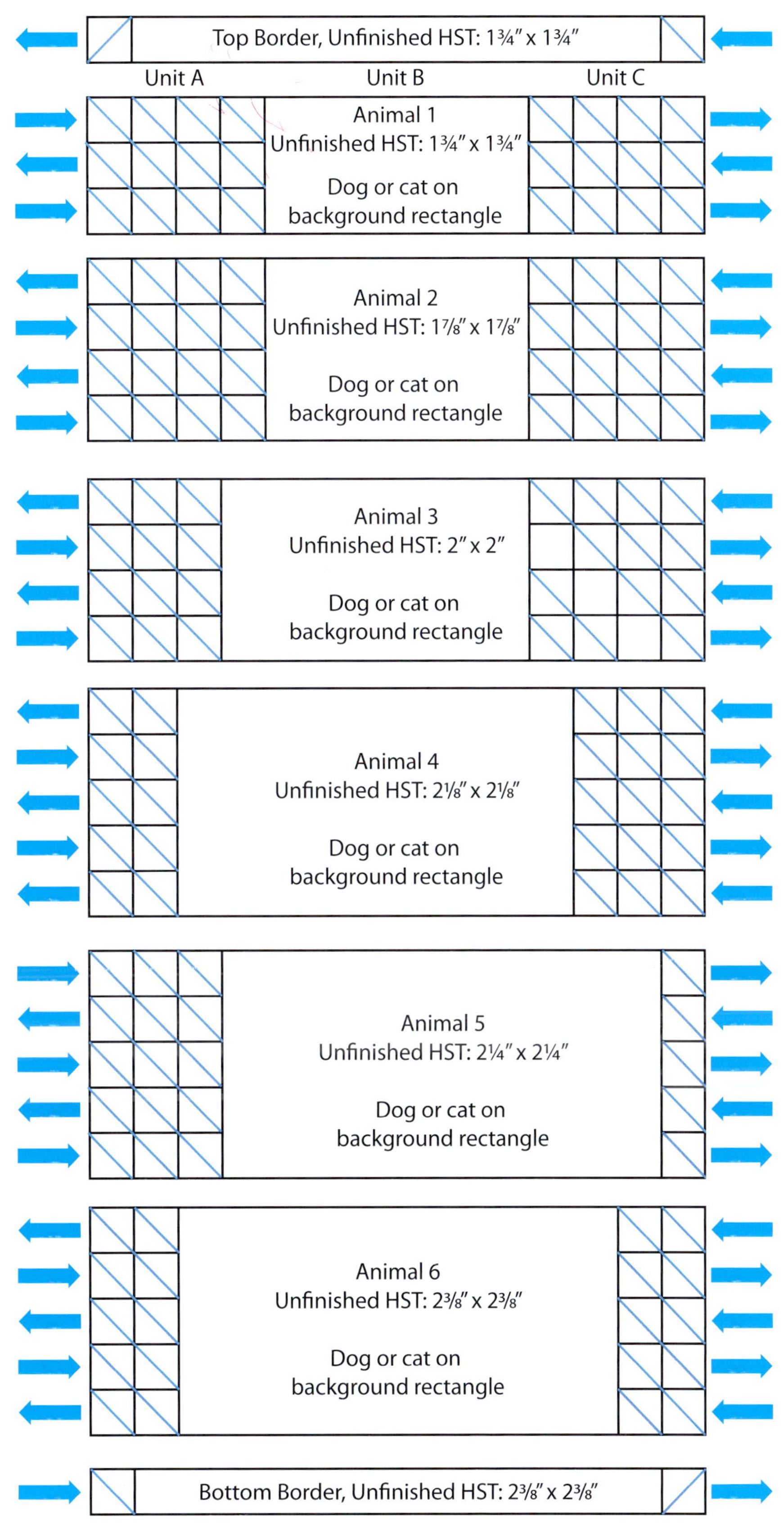

Piecing Diagram (arrows indicate pressing direction)

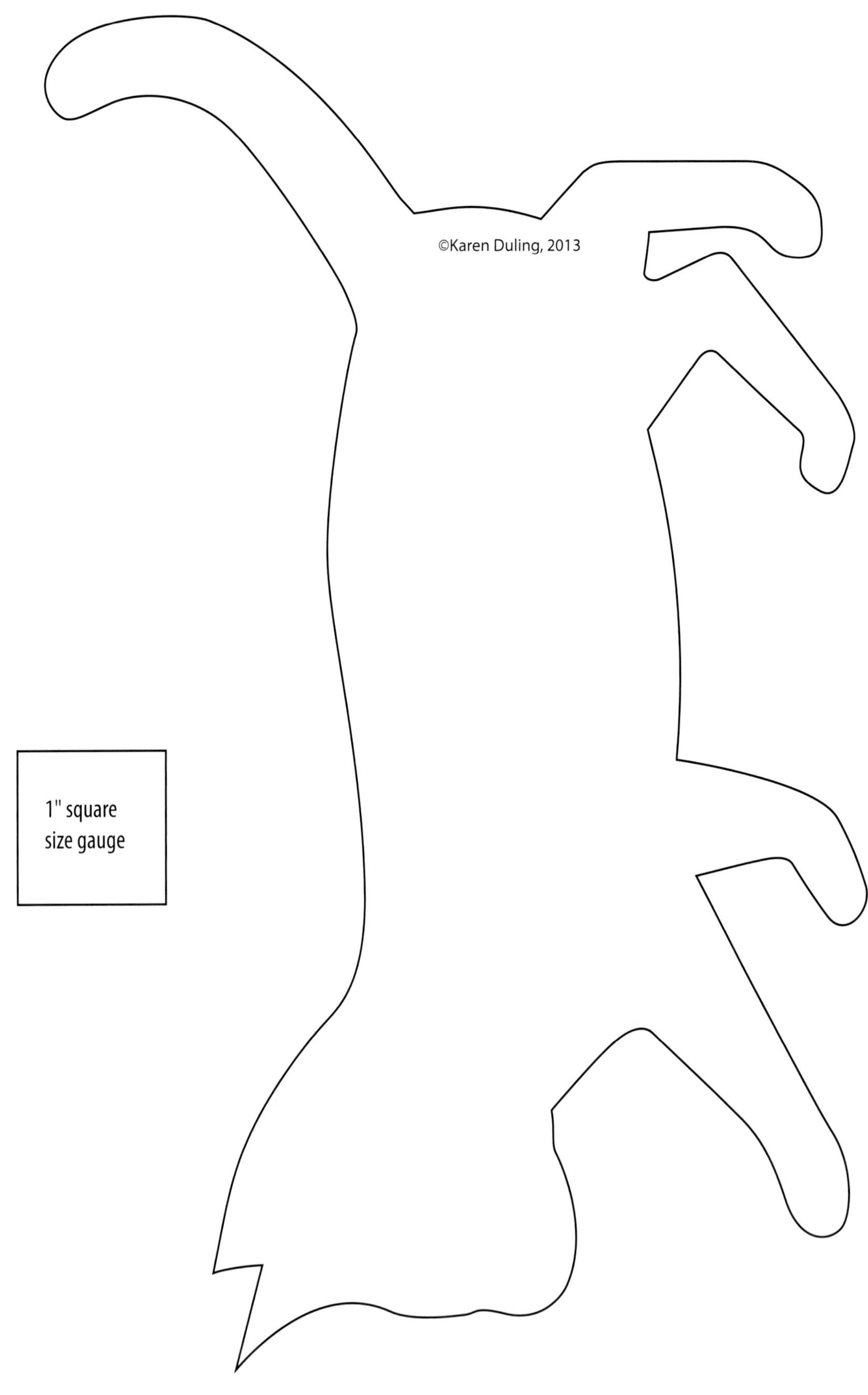

©Karen Duling, 2013
1" square
size gauge

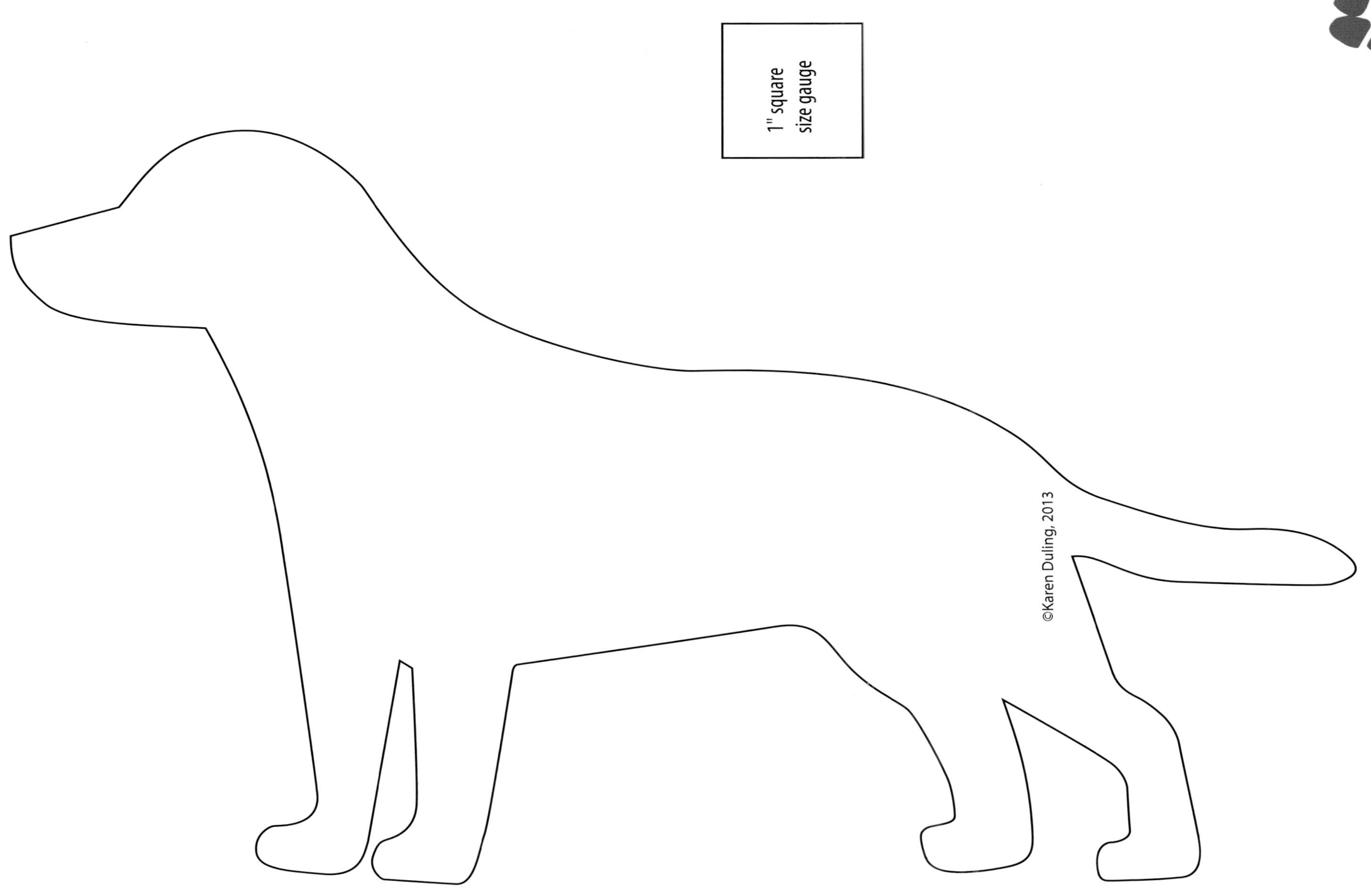

1" square
size gauge

©Karen Duling, 2013

Polka Dogs: Lap-Size Project

Polka Dogs, 57" x 72", made by the author. Machine quilting by Nancy Boyse, East Lansing, Michigan.

Karen Duling

PATTERN INSPIRATION

I set out to design a "modular" pattern, where dog parts could be rearranged to form different canine shapes, reflecting the wide variety of dogs found at animal shelters. The result is POLKA DOGS. Four different head styles, four different tail styles, and one "universal" body are sewn together to make twelve unique dogs. A funky angled border surrounds the somewhat crooked, dancing dogs.

YARDAGE REQUIREMENTS

Neutral #1 for background and border filler	1½ yards
Neutral #2 for background for the middle body unit	½ yard
Brown dog fabric	1½ yards
Ear flap fabric and border filler (chartreuse in the sample)	⅜ yard
Light polka dot fabric for block sashing and border filler	1⅜ yards
Dark polka dot for block sashing and border filler	1⅛ yards
Brown stripe for inner border	⅓ yard
Contrast fabric for border filler (orange, brown, and yellow fabrics are used in the sample)	½ yard
Binding	⅝ yard
Backing	3⅞ yards
Batting	65" x 80"

CUTTING THE BLOCKS

Cut the number of pieces of each color as shown in the chart below.

The squares in the rows marked with an asterisk (*) are for making the HSTs (page 4). See the HST chart on page 16 for the numbers and combinations needed.

As you are cutting your fabrics, sort by letter, then by size, then by color according to the letter identifier shown in the first column of the chart. This will make assembly into the head, tail, and body units much easier.

	Size	Neutral #1	Neutral #2	Brown Dog Fabric	Chartreuse Ear Fabric
A	1½" x 1½"	3		18	3
B	1½" x 2½"	24		15	
C	1½" x 3½"		12	6	
D	1½" x 4½"	3		18	
E	1½" x 5½"	18		6	
F	1½" x 6½"			9	
*For HSTs	1⅞" x 1⅞"	24	6	32	5
G	2½" x 2½"	9		9	3
H	2½" x 3½"	3			
I	2½" x 4½"	3	12	6	
J	2½" x 5½"	6			
K	2½" x 7½"			9	
*For HSTs	2⅞" x 2⅞"	14		15	2
L	3½" x 4½"		12		
M	3½" x 5½"	6		3	
N	3½" x 6½"	6			
O	3½" x 7½"	6			
*For HSTs	3⅞" x 3⅞"	2		2	
P	4½" x 5½"	3		12	
Q	4½" x 6½"	3			
*For HSTs	4⅞" x 4⅞"	2		2	

Piecing Diagrams

White = neutral #1 background fabric
Yellow = ear flap fabric—chartreuse
Orange = neutral #2 background fabric
Pink = dog body fabric—brown

Press horizontal seams down on head and tail units.
Press horizontal seams up on body unit.

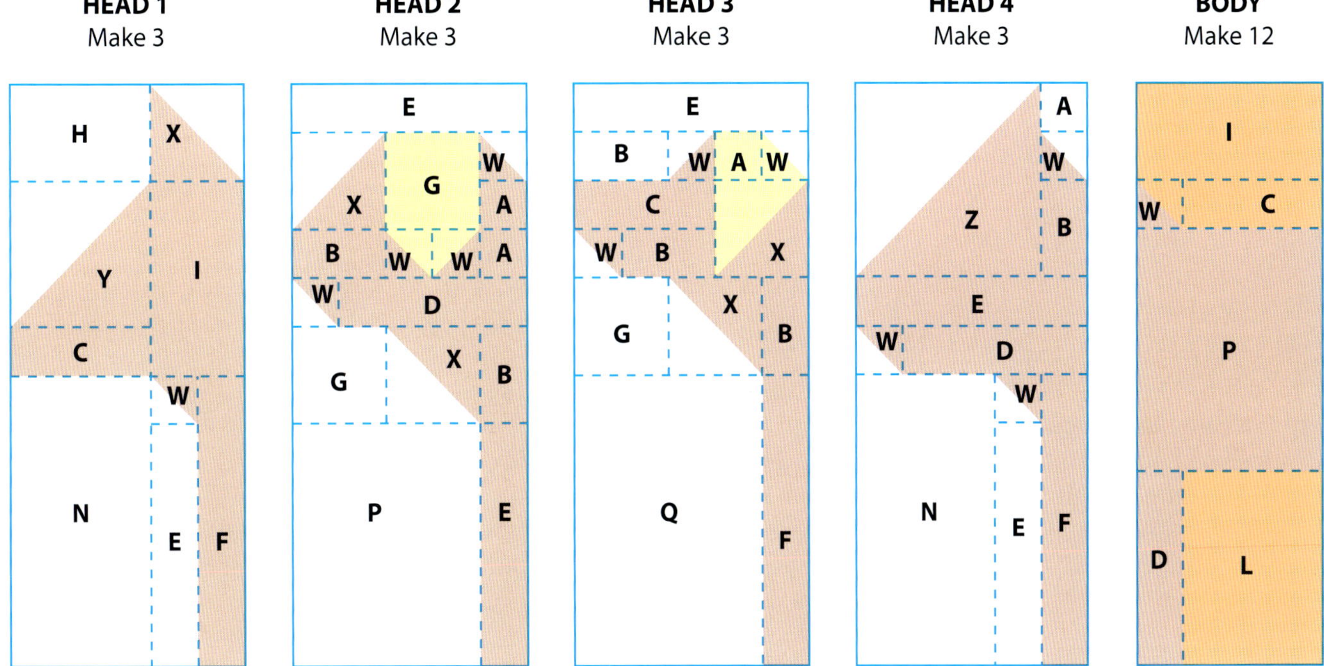

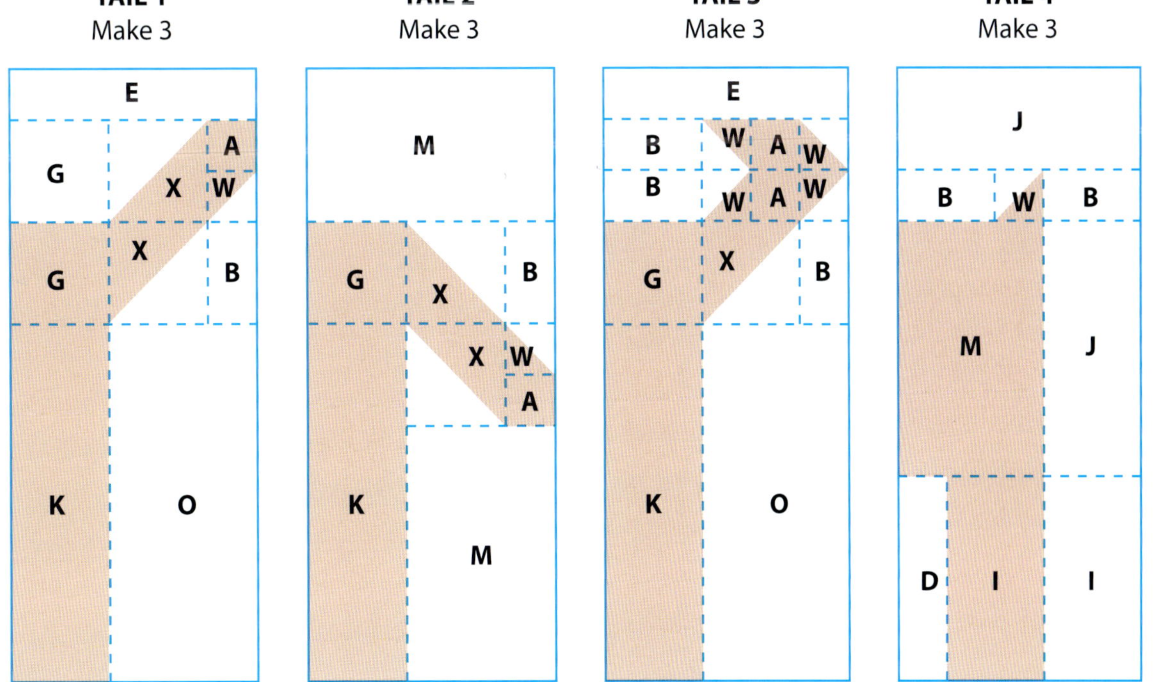

CUTTING THE SASHING, BORDERS, AND BINDING

Sashing and Pieced Border:

Size	Dark Polka Dot	Light Polka Dot	Contrast Fabric	Neutral Fabric	Chartreuse
3¼" x 12½"	12				
3¼" x 17¼"	12				
3¼" x 15¼"		12			
3¼" x 20"		12			
3¼" x 15"	2	2	6	4	6

Inner border: 6 – 1½" strips
Binding: 7 – 2¼" strips

SEWING INSTRUCTIONS

STEP 1: Assemble the squares (rows marked with * in the chart on page 14) into half-square triangle units (HSTs) using the fabric combinations shown below. The units become the lettered pieces indicated.

STEP 2: Stack and sort the HSTs by letter (W, X, Y, and Z), size, and color.

STEP 3: Assemble and sew parts together according to the pattern for each head, tail, and body unit (page 15).

Number of HST units needed:

	Cut Size (Unfinished size including seam allowance)	Neutral #1 & Brown	Neutral #1 & Chartreuse	Neutral #2 & Brown	Brown & Chartreuse
W	1⅞" x 1⅞" (1½" x 1½")	45	3	12	6
X	2⅞" x 2⅞" (2½" x 2½")	27			3
Y	3⅞" x 3⅞" (3½" x 3½")	3			
Z	4⅞" x 4⅞" (4½" x 4½")	3			

Starting with the first dog head style, lay out pieces for 3 units. Sew pieces together in rows, alternating the direction of the pressed vertical seams in each row. Then sew the rows together to make 3 complete head units.

In the same way, make 3 units of each of the 4 tail styles and 12 body units.

Step 4: Mix and match the units until you have 12 complete dogs. Join 3 units for each dog.

Step 5: Sew sashing strips to the blocks in the sequence indicated. Press after you add each strip, pressing seams away from the dog (**Fig. 4**).

Step 6: Trim each block to measure 16" x 16". Using a large square quilter's ruler or see-through plastic template, place the square on the sashed block, and rotate it so that the dog is either leaning left or right. Be careful not to cut off a corner of the neutral background fabric by rotating too much. Remember that the seam line will be ¼" inside the 16" square. Vary the direction and amount of the tilt for each block. Measure twice, cut once! Cut along the edge of the ruler or template. Save the trimmed sashing scraps for the angled border (**Fig. 5**).

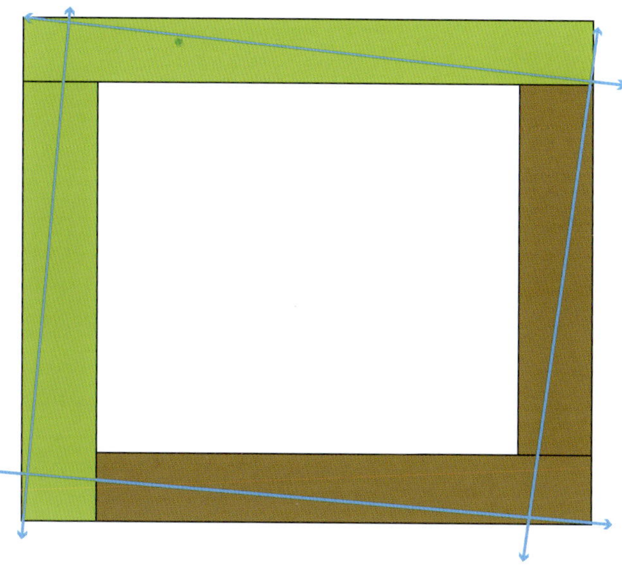

Fig. 5

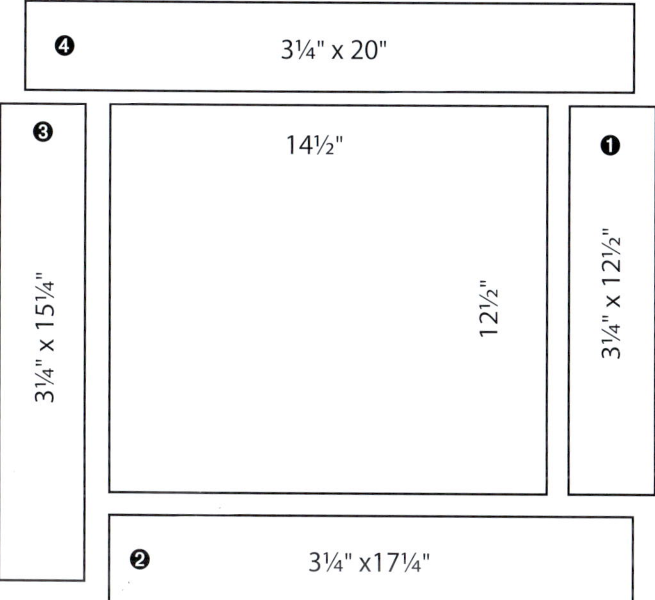

❹ 3¼" x 20"

❸ 14½" ❶

3¼" x 15¼" 12½" 3¼" x 12½"

❷ 3¼" x17¼"

Fig. 4

Merle's Tips!

Since your sashed dog blocks and sashing scraps have bias edges, be careful when sewing them as the edges will be stretchier than those cut on the straight grain of the fabric.

Step 7: Arrange the blocks to your liking in four rows of three blocks each. Join the blocks into rows, and then sew the rows together.

Step 8: Join inner border fabric strips together, end to end, and press the seams open. Sew to the sides of the quilt (page 4).

STEP 9: Cut the 3¼" x 15" rectangles on an "almost" diagonal—that is, not directly from corner to corner. Stay at least 1" from the corner on the short edges of the rectangles when cutting the diagonal, always slicing through the short ends (FIG. 6).

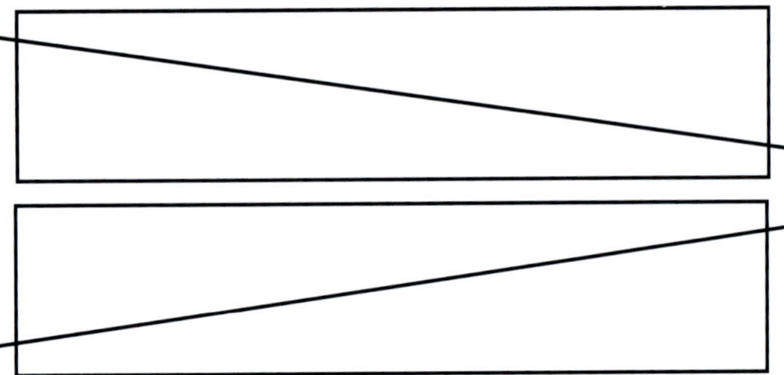

FIG. 6

Cut the sashing scraps to a length of 15", measuring along the straight grain. (Some sashing scraps may not be usable if they are less than ¾" at either end.) Add the cut rectangle pieces, mix them all up, and sew together in pairs from bias edge to bias edge, creating new "almost" rectangles. Trim one long edge so the two long edges are parallel, creating true rectangles as shown below (FIG. 7).

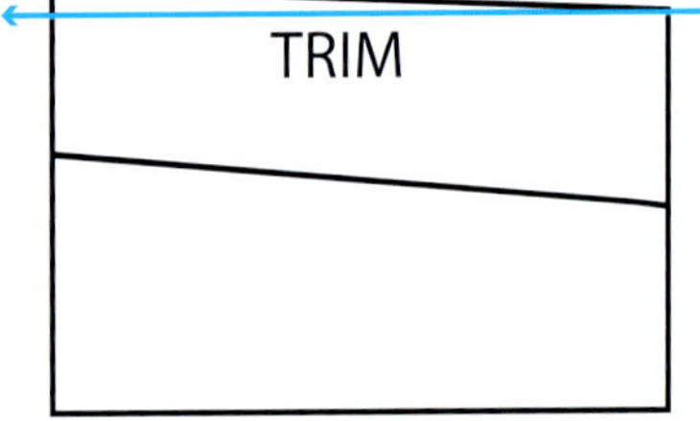

FIG. 7

STEP 10: Sew the rectangles together along the long edges into long strip-sets. Cut the strip-sets at right angles to the seam lines into three 4¼" wide strip-sets, as shown (FIG. 8).

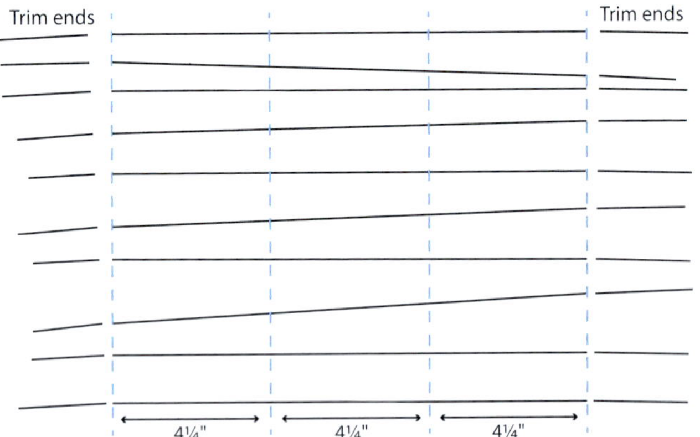

FIG. 8

Sew the 4¼" sets together, from short edge to short edge, as needed to border the quilt. You need approximately 245" of 4¼" wide borders.

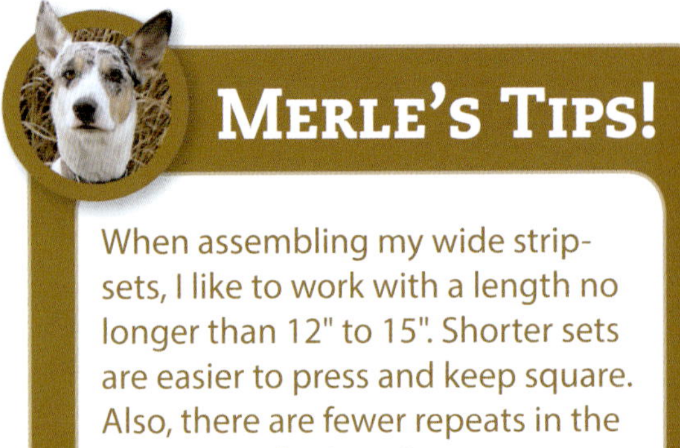

When assembling my wide strip-sets, I like to work with a length no longer than 12" to 15". Shorter sets are easier to press and keep square. Also, there are fewer repeats in the sequence of colors. Square-up your strip-sets as you go along, as things can easily go astray.

STEP 11: Sew the pieced borders to the sides of quilt (page 4).

STEP 12: Assemble the quilt layers and quilt as desired.

FUN IDEAS TO CONSIDER

Put sweaters on your dogs by using fabric scraps. Simply substitute these scraps for piece "P" in the body unit (page 15).

Make scrappy dogs. Most of the dog head, tail, and body pieces are small, and would be perfect for using up scraps.

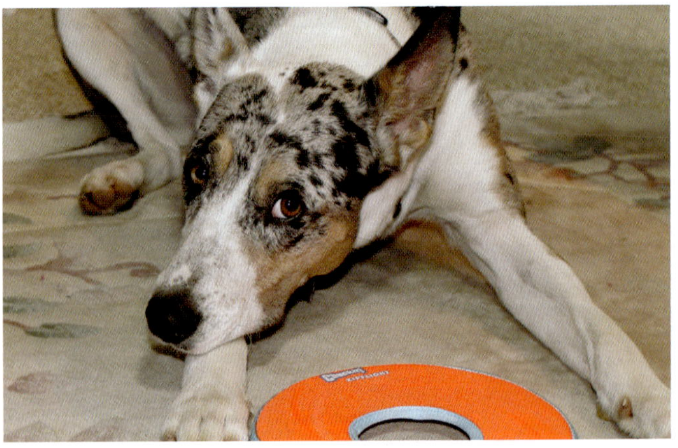

Is it time to play frisbee?

DOG NATION, 55" x 69", made by the author using stash scraps.

CAT TAILS, 73" x 98" (twin size), made by the author. Machine quilting by Wendy Paskus, East Lansing, Michigan.

PATTERN INSPIRATION

The essence of a cat or dog can be captured by using the tail profile: Happy tails, sad tails, and "Sorry I ate the bread on the counter" tails. Tails are the inspiration for this series of quilts.

My first tail quilt was made at the request of my friend, Paula Clegg, to make a charity quilt. I sketched an image of a dog tail and asked her if that was something she liked. She did, so I began collecting paw-print fabrics and made the quilt in earth tones. It was the one that started it all—the fabric collecting, the charity quilts, and the keepsake blocks for pet owners who had suffered a loss. It remains my favorite pattern.

YARDAGE REQUIREMENTS

Yardage requirements, cutting instructions, and assembly are the same whether you use the dog or cat tail pattern. Simply choose your tail pattern (pages 29 & 30) and quilt size and start creating.

Read through all instructions before cutting. Twin and throw instructions start on page 23; mini size instructions start on page 27.

Quilt Dimensions	Twin 73" x 98"	Throw 50" x 50"	Mini 23" x 23"
Main fabrics for blocks, tails, and patched border. Choosing light and dark fabrics as well as medium-value fabrics is important. Use one or more paw-print, dog-bone, or other pet-themed fabric to add whimsy to your project.	⅞ yard each of 9 fabrics 1⅛ yards of a 10th fabric (9 yards total)	½ yard each of 6 fabrics (3 yards total)	½ yard light background ⅓ yard gray tail fabric ¼ yard each of 6 border fabrics (Choose a medium and dark value for each of 3 colors—1½ yards total.)
Inner and outer borders	2 yards	1⅛ yards	
Border corner squares	¼ yard	¼ yard	(4) 3⅜" squares (4) 2¾" squares for hearts
Double-fold straight-grain binding	¾ yard	½ yard	¼ yard
Backing (pieced) See Merle's Tips.	6 yards	3⅜ yards	⅞ yard
9" x 12" sheets of paper backed-fusible	14 sheets	4 sheets	2 sheets
Batting	81" x 106"	58" x 58"	31" x 31"

MERLE'S TIPS!

I wait to buy my backing fabric until my top is completed. Then, after a survey of the scraps that remain, I sew them together to use as part of the yardage for the pieced back. This helps keep the scrap pile from getting out of control!

CUTTING INSTRUCTIONS

All strips are cut selvage to selvage.

FABRIC TYPE	PLACEMENT	TWIN	THROW	MINI
Main fabrics	Blocks and tails	81 squares Cut (2) 8½" strips from each of the 10 fabrics into 4 squares 8½" x 8½". Cut 1 additional square from the tenth fabric.	24 squares From each of the 6 fabrics, cut (1) 8½" strip into 4 squares each.	4 squares From light background fabric and gray tail fabric, cut from each one, (1) 8" strip, then cut into 4 squares.
	Patched border	40 strips For the Sixteen-Patch border, cut (4) 2" strips of each of the 10 fabrics.	12 strips For the Four-Patch border, cut (2) 2" strips of each of the 6 fabrics.	16 strips For the chevron border, cut (2) 1½" strips from each of 6 fabrics. From the light background fabric, cut (4) 1½" strips.
Corner squares	Sixteen Patch border corners	Cut 4 squares 5" x 5" from the tenth fabric.		
	Inner border corners	4 squares 3½" x 3½"	4 squares 2½" x 2½"	
	Outer border corners	4 squares 4¼" x 4¼"	4 squares 4¼" x 4¼"	4 squares 3⅜" x 3⅜" 4 hearts 2¾" x 2¾"
Inner and outer borders	Inner	(7) 3½" strips	(4) 2½" strips	
	Outer	(8) 4¼" strips	(5) 4¼" strips	
Binding		(9) 2¼" strips	(6) 2¼" strips	(3) 2¼" strips

Karen Duling

Dog Tails, 50" x 50" (throw size), made by the author. Machine quilting by Nancy Boyse, East Lansing, Michigan.

Sewing Instructions for Twin and Throw Sizes

Step 1: Sort the 8½" squares into sets of 3 different fabrics each. One set of 3 squares will make 2 complete tail blocks. For each group determine which will be the A, B, or C square. Square A is cut into two pieces, a tail (A-1), which is placed atop square B, and the background of a tail (A-2), which is placed atop square C. Lighter fabrics are best as B or C squares, as they will not shadow through the fused tail shapes.

Step 2: Trace the dog or cat tail pattern onto the template material of your choice. Cut out on the drawn line. The tail template will be a reverse of the finished image.

STEP 3: Place the tail template on the wrong side of each Square A, matching the lower left corners. In the seam allowance, mark where the body lines meet the edges of the square, using a fabric marking pencil (FIG. 9). Set aside.

FIG. 9. Placement marks on tail square A

STEP 4: Place the template on the paper side of a sheet of paper-backed fusible web. Trace around the template with a pencil. (Two tails will fit on each 9" x 12" sheet.) Repeat, tracing the number of shapes needed for your size quilt (FIG. 10).

FIG. 10. Fusible sheet layout

STEP 5: Working one tail at a time, cut a rough ¼" to ⅜" INSIDE the traced line. Then, cut a rough ¼" to ⅜" OUTSIDE the traced line (FIG. 11).

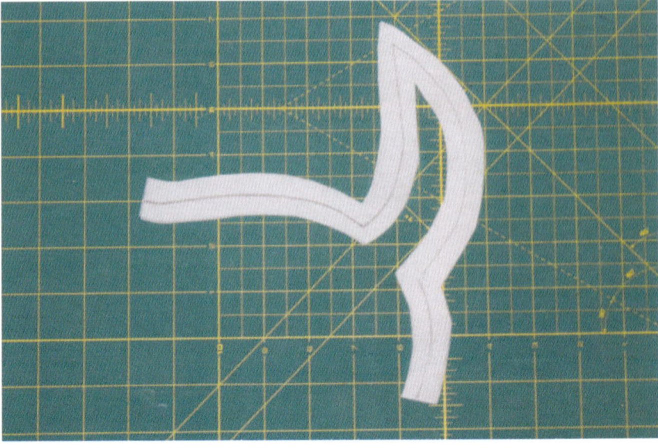

FIG. 11. Cut out the fusible shape.

STEP 6: With the sticky, fusible side of the tail shape facing the WRONG side of fabric square A, match the marked placement lines. Smooth the tail shape atop the square. Fuse in place following the manufacturer's instruction (FIG. 12).

FIG. 12. Fuse to the back of tail square A.

MERLE'S TIPS!

For tail templates, I use template plastic sheets sold at craft stores. A sheet of freezer paper ironed to the back of a piece of copy paper makes a nice stiff template and works equally well.

My favorite fusible web, Lite Steam-A-Seam 2, has a paper lining designed to come away easily. Don't trace on this liner; use the paper on the other side, which is backed with sticky web fusing. The liner can be removed before or after tracing, whichever method works best for you.

Karen Duling

STEP 7: Carefully cut out the fabric tail shape along the traced line, resulting in pieces A-1 and A-2 (FIG. 13A).

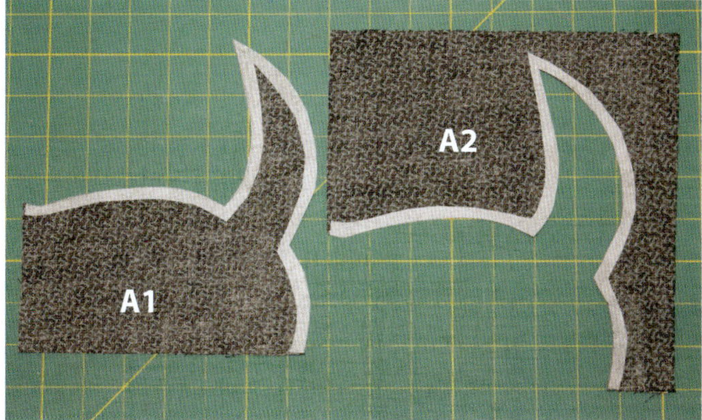

FIG. 13A. Cut out A-1 and A-2 tail shapes on the traced line.

Turn right-side up (FIG. 13B).

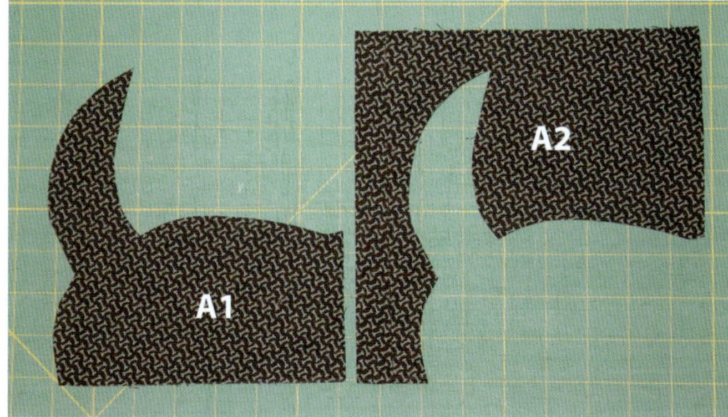

FIG. 13B.

STEP 8: Peel the paper from A-1 and place the WRONG side of the tail on the RIGHT side of square B, matching the corner and edges. Similarly, position the A-2 shape onto square C. Make sure fusible web does not extend past edges of the block. Fuse in place. Repeat steps 5–8 for all the squares (FIG. 14).

FIG. 14. Place the A-1 piece (the tail) on square B and the A-2 piece (the tail background) on square C.

STEP 9: With the completed blocks right-side up, fold back the top layer of the fabric and carefully slice off the extra bottom layer of fabric from the corners (FIG. 15).

FIG. 15. Trim the under layer of fabric.

The fusible tail shape will be sticky on one side. Smooth each cutout onto the tail fabric squares as you go to avoid a sticky tangle of tails. Trim fusible edges to keep them from going over edges of the square. Be careful to keep the sticky adhesive off of your iron and ironing surface!

Step 10: Machine appliqué along the tail edge (page 4).

Step 11: Lay out the blocks in rows. Adjust the block placement until you are happy with the arrangement. Join the blocks into rows, pressing vertical seams in the opposite direction of the row before. Then sew the rows together.

Step 12: Sew the inner border to the quilt, adding the corner squares (page 4).

Step 13: Sew the 2" strips cut for the patched borders into strip-sets as shown. Press the seams toward the darker strips. See figure 16 for the twin size or figure 19 for the throw size.

Step 14: Cut the strip-sets into the required number of 2" segments (FIG. 16 OR 19).

TWIN SIZE

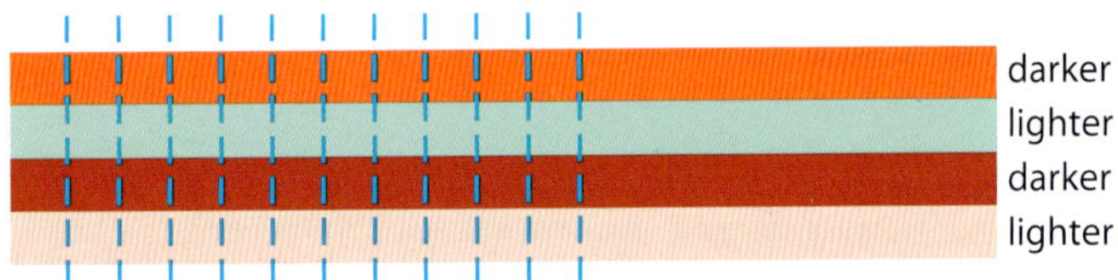

FIG. 16. Make 10 strip-sets of 4 strips each. Cut 184 - 2" segments.

Join the segments into pairs, then sew the pairs together to form 44 Sixteen-Patch blocks (FIG. 17). You'll have 8 segments left over.

FIG. 17. Make 44 Sixteen-Patch blocks.

To make the corner blocks, remove one square from 4 of the remaining 8 segments. Add a three-square segment to one side of a 5" x 5" square. Add the four-square segment to the adjacent side. Make 4 (FIG. 18).

Join 13 blocks for the side borders. Add to the quilt. Join 9 blocks and 2 corner blocks for the top and bottom borders. Add to the quilt.

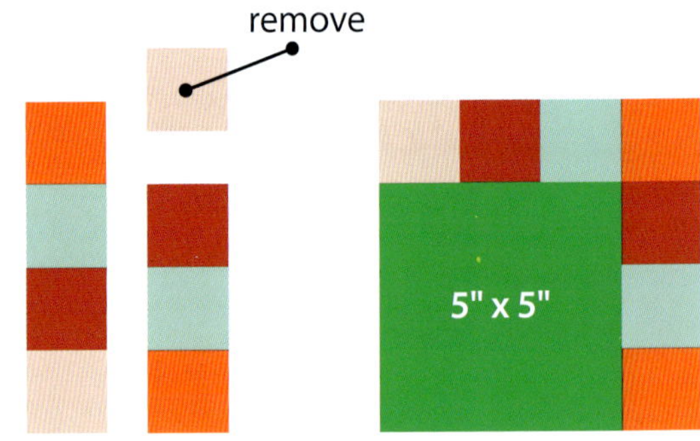

FIG. 18. Make 4 corner blocks.

THROW SIZE

FIG. 19. Make 6 strip-sets of 2 strips each. Cut 104 - 2" segments.

Combine and sew segment pairs to form 52 Four-Patch blocks (FIG. 20). Join 12 blocks for the side borders. Add to the sides. Join 14 blocks for the top and bottom borders. Add to the quilt.

FIG. 20. Make 52 Four-Patch blocks.

Step 15: Sew outer borders and outer border corner squares to the quilt.

Step 16: Assemble quilt layers and quilt as desired.

MINI SIZE

STEP 1: Follow the instructions for Twin and Throw sizes, Step 2 through Step 11 (pages 23–26). The tail fabric squares will be Square A, and cut to become tail piece A-1. Four background squares will be square B. Pieces A-2 and square C are not used in the mini size, so disregard references to those pieces.

STEP 2: Sew the 1½" strips cut for the patched border into strip-sets as shown.

Make 2 strip-sets of 4 strips each in both combinations (**FIG. 21**).

Lighter chevrons—press all seams down

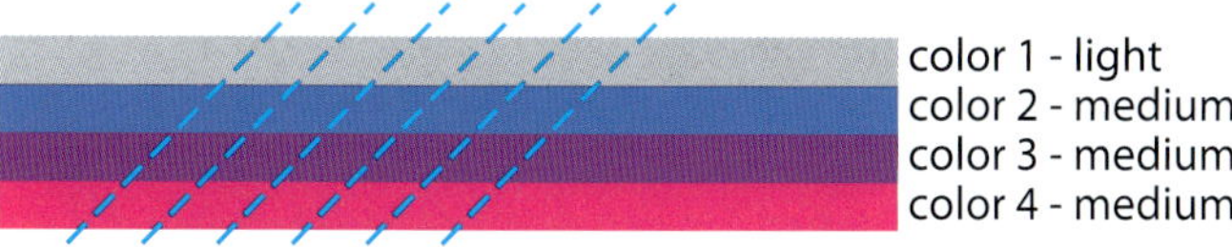

Make 2 strip-sets.

Darker chevrons—press all seams up

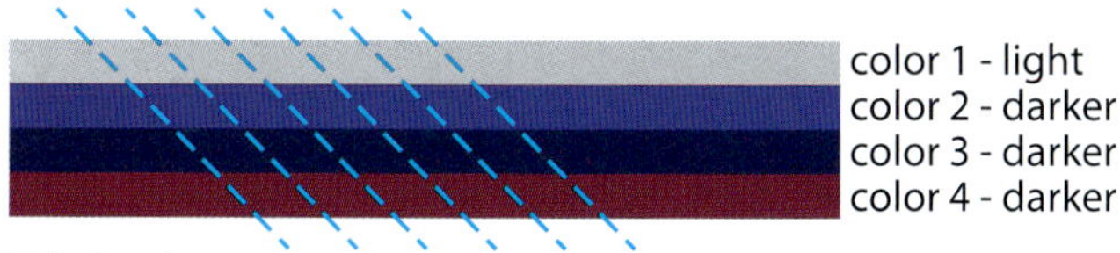

Make 2 strip-sets.

FIG. 21

STEP 3: Cut each strip-set into 2" chevron segments by cutting at a 45-degree angle to the seam lines (**FIG. 22**).

Fig. 22. Cut segments at a 45-degree angle.

HEARTS OF GOLD, 23" x 23" (mini size), made by the author

STEP 4: Sew 10 chevron segments together for each side border (**FIG. 23**). Start each border with a dark chevron segment with the light fabric piece at the top, alternating dark and lighter slices. (Extra segments will be used in corner squares.)

Fig. 23. Alternate the light and dark segments.

FOR GRACE, 11½" x 11¼", made by the author. Letter patterns not included.

STEP 5: Trim each border to a width of 4¾", leaving ¼" seam allowance from peaks, as shown (**FIG. 24**).

FIG. 24. Trim the pieced border strips.

STEP 6: To make the corner squares, remove the light piece from 4 light and 4 dark chevron segments as shown (**FIG. 25**).

Fig. 25. Remove the top light piece.

Sew the dark segment on the left of the corner square and lighter segment on top using a Y-seam (**FIG. 26**).

FIG. 26. Add the shortened segments to the corner squares. Trim. Make 4.

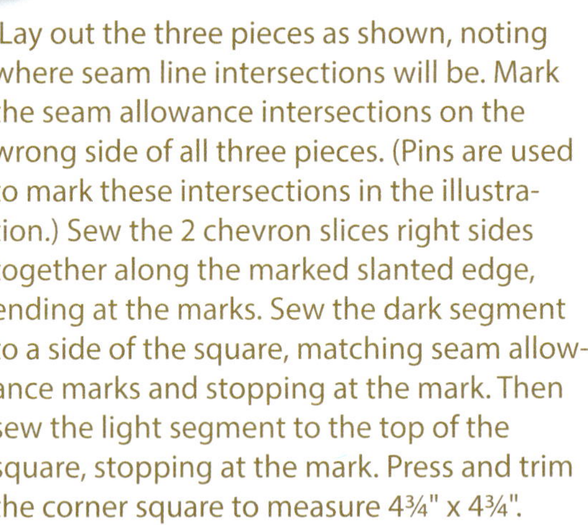

MERLE'S TIPS!

Lay out the three pieces as shown, noting where seam line intersections will be. Mark the seam allowance intersections on the wrong side of all three pieces. (Pins are used to mark these intersections in the illustration.) Sew the 2 chevron slices right sides together along the marked slanted edge, ending at the marks. Sew the dark segment to a side of the square, matching seam allowance marks and stopping at the mark. Then sew the light segment to the top of the square, stopping at the mark. Press and trim the corner square to measure 4¾" x 4¾".

STEP 7: Sew the borders and corner squares to quilt (page 4).

STEP 8: Trace 4 heart shapes (page 30) onto fusible web. Cut ¼" on the OUTSIDE of the traced line and ¼" INSIDE the line. Fuse to the wrong side of the heart fabric square. Cut out on the traced line. Remove the paper, place the hearts on the corner squares, and fuse. Machine appliqué around the hearts (page 4).

STEP 9: Assemble quilt layers and quilt as desired.

Use dotted line for mini-size quilt.

©Karen Duling, 2013

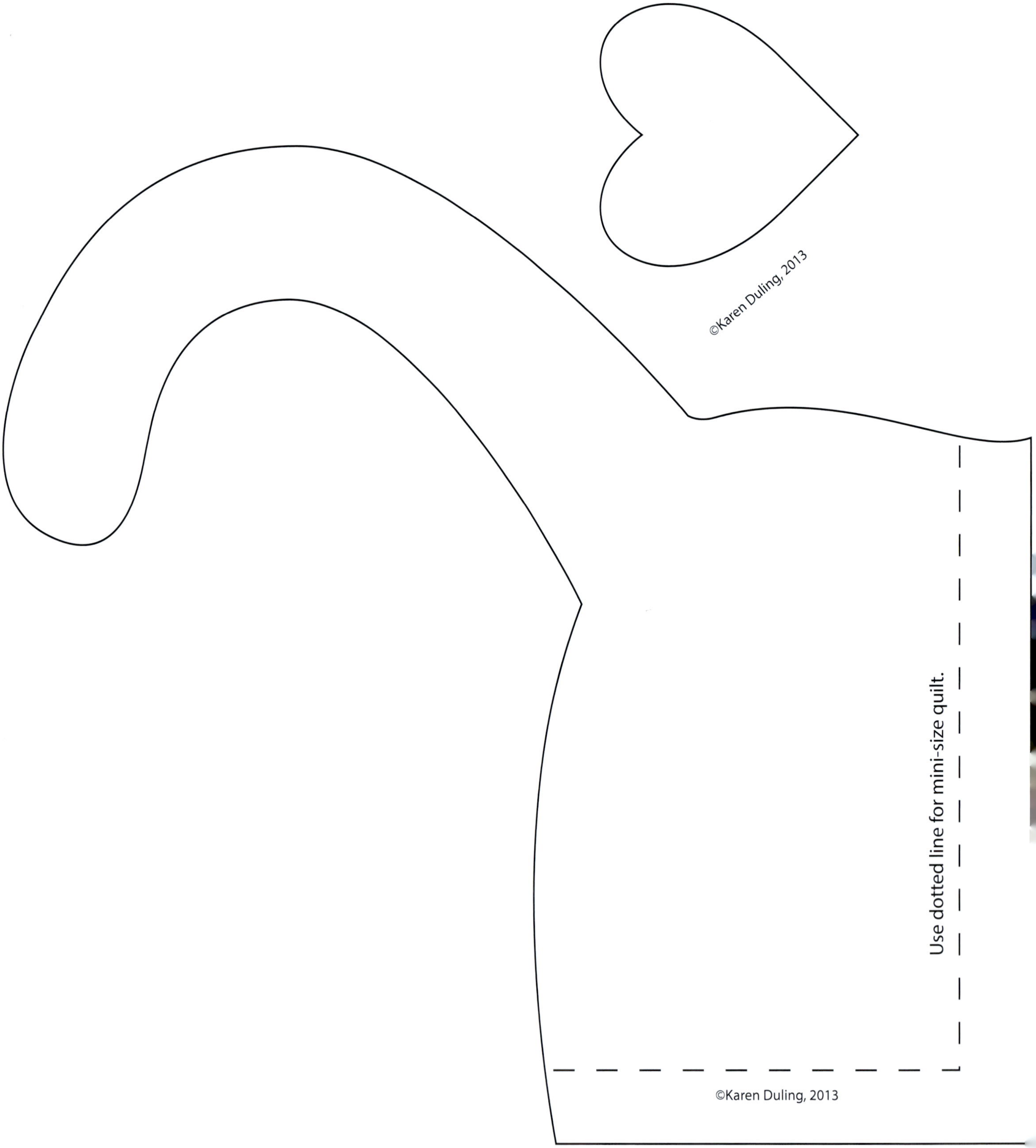

©Karen Duling, 2013

Use dotted line for mini-size quilt.

©Karen Duling, 2013

 Karen Duling

MEET KAREN DULING

Karen lives in mid-Michigan with her husband, Linn, and dog, Merle. Two grown children have left the nest but provide Merle with more youthful playmates during their visits home.

Karen is a graduate of the University of Michigan (Go Blue!). After a career in state government in water quality programs, quilting has become her passion. She began sewing as a young girl and focused her sewing on clothing until she was introduced to quilting twenty years ago by her sister, Cindy Bowker.

She has enjoyed many pets throughout her life—a tightrope-walking mouse, Whitey the Mighty; turtles named Buzz and Chipper; a one-legged singing parakeet, Crosby, who could whistle the University of Michigan fight song; numerous tropical fish; dogs Buddy, Caesar, and Merle; cats Pookey, Oliver, Kitty, Boots, Rocco, Katy, and Grace.

Karen is an enthusiastic collector of animal-themed fabrics. Many of her quilts are donated to benefit charity causes. She hopes that you will be inspired to do the same. Her work was featured in the August 2012 issue of *The Quilt Life* magazine.

Learn more about Karen at: www.karendulingquilts.com .

More AQS Books

This is only a small selection of the books available from the American Quilter's Society. AQS books are known worldwide for timely topics, clear writing, beautiful color photos, and accurate illustrations and patterns. The following books are available from your local bookseller, quilt shop, or public library.

#1585 .... $12.95

#1586 .... $12.95

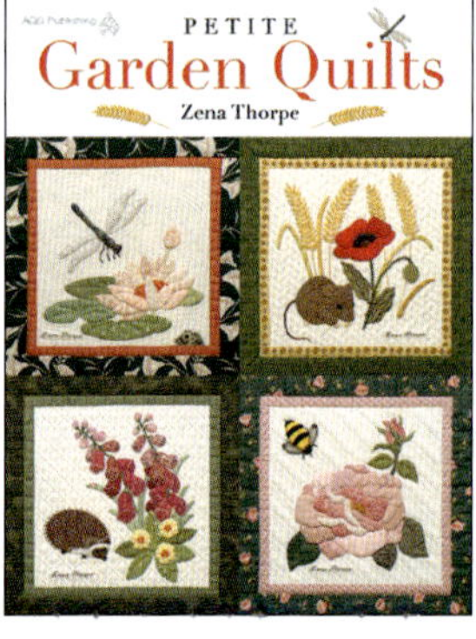

#1590 .... $12.95

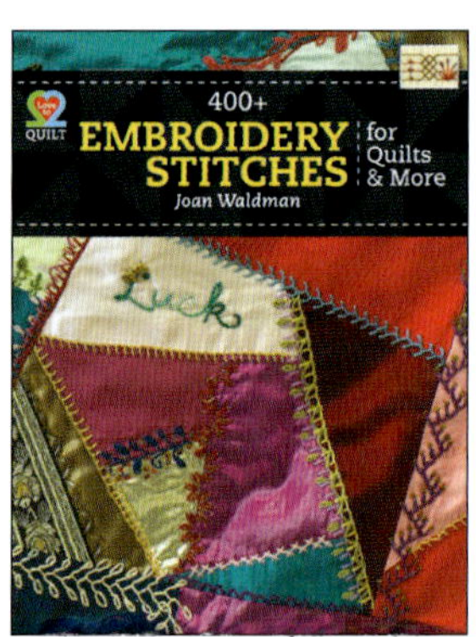

#1274 .... $12.95

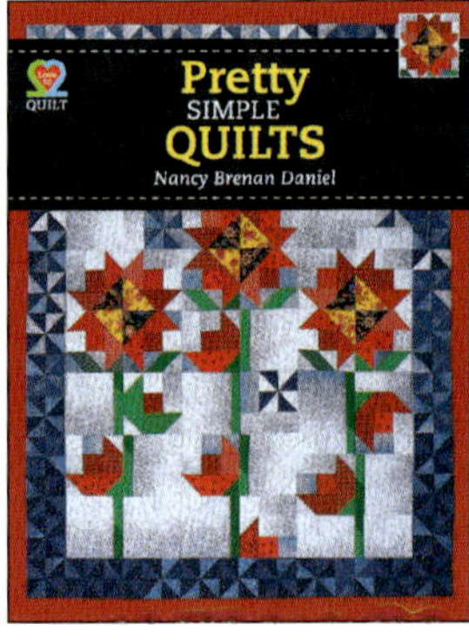

#1278 .... $12.95

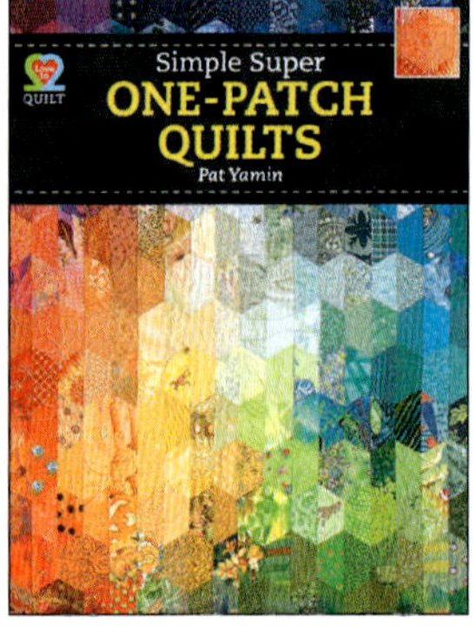

#1275 .... $12.95

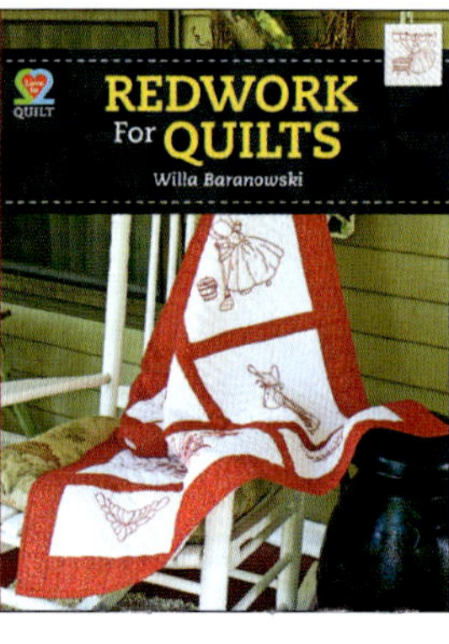

#1273 .... $12.95

#1589 .... $12.95

LOOK for these books nationally.
CALL or **VISIT** our website at

1-800-626-5420
www.AmericanQuilter.com